Handy Nevada Genealogy Handbook

Gary L. Morris

©2015 Gary L. Morris

ISBN-13: 978-1507787267

ISBN-10: 150778726X

Table of Contents

Notes

Genealogical Research in Nevada

There are many genealogical records and resources available for tracing your family history in Nevada. Because there are so many records held at many different locations, tracking down the records for your ancestor can be an ominous task. Don't worry though, we know just where they are, and we'll show you which records you'll need, while helping you to understand:

1. What they are
2. Where to find them
3. How to use them

These records can be found both online and off, so we'll introduce you to online websites, indexes and databases, as well as brick-and-mortar repositories and other institutions that will help with your research in Nevada. So that you will have a more comprehensive understanding of these records, we have provided a brief history of the "Silver State" to illustrate what type of records may have been generated during specific time periods. That information will assist you in pinpointing times and locations on which to focus the search for your Nevada ancestors and their records.

A Brief History of Nevada

Native Americans have inhabited Nevada for 12,000 years or so. The major tribes living there today are the Northern and Southern Paiute, Shoshoni, and the Washo. It is believed the first white European to visit the region was Spanish priest Francisco Garces, who it is thought penetrated extreme southern Nevada in 1776. In 1826 Peter Skene Ogden of the British Hudson's Bay Company entered the northeast and later explored the Humboldt River. Rival American trapper Jedediah Smith traversed the state in 1826–27, followed by John C. Frémont in 1843.

The Mormons founded the first permanent white settlement at Mormon Station (later Genoa), in 1850, and other settlements soon followed, especially in Las Vegas Valley. When large deposits of silver were discovered in 1859, hoards of prospectors from California flocked to the area. Nevada became a separate territory in 1861, and achieved statehood three years later. The gold and silver deposits at the Comstock Lode accelerated the economic prosperity of Nevada until the late 1870's when the ore deposits were exhausted.

After a more than twenty year slump, Nevada's economy was revived when silver and gold were discovered at Tonopah and Goldfield respectively. Copper discoveries in eastern Nevada further bolstered the revival, until the 1920's when mining fell off. During this period Nevada established itself as a divorce destination, but the economy didn't fully recover until the gaming became the state's principal industry in the 1950's.

Important Dates in Nevada History

1776 – Claimed by France

1821 – Claimed by Mexico

1848 – Acquired by the United States from Mexico in the Treaty of Guadalupe- Hidalgo

1850 – First permanent settlement established by Mormons

1858 – Carson City established

1859 – Silver discovered at Comstock Lode

1860 – Over 10,000 settlers come from California to prospect for gold and silver

1861 – Created as separate territory

1864 – Statehood

1906 – Copper discovered

1931 – Gambling legalized, first casino the Pair-O-Dice Club built

Famous Battles Fought in Nevada

White settlers in Nevada had their share of conflict with the Native American Tribes which eventually culminated in the **Paiute War** in 1860.

Paiute War: http://www.militarymuseum.org/PyramidLake.html

These battle accounts that exist can be very effective in uncovering the military records of your ancestor. They can tell you what regiments fought in which battles, and often include the names and ranks of many officers and enlisted men.

Common Nevada Genealogical Issues and Resources to Overcome Them

Boundary Changes: Boundary changes are a common obstacle when researching Nevada ancestors. You could be searching for an ancestor's record in one county when in fact it is stored in a different one due to historical county boundary changes.

The **Atlas of Historical County Boundaries** can help you to overcome that problem. It provides a chronological listing of every boundary change that has occurred in the history of Nevada.

Atlas of Historical County Boundaries:
http://publications.newberry.org/ahcbp/documents/NV_Consolidated _Chronology.htm#Consolidated_Chronology

Name Changes: Surname changes, variations, and misspellings can complicate genealogical research. It is important to check all spelling variations. Soundex, a program that indexes names by sound, is a useful first step, but you can't rely on it completely as some name variations result in different Soundex codes. The surnames could be different, but the first name may be different too. You can also find records filed under initials, middle names, and nicknames as well, so you will need to **get creative with surname variations** and spellings in order to cover all the possibilities. For help with surname variations read our instructional article on **How to Use Soundex**.

get creative with surname variations:
http://obituarieshelp.org/blog/?p=634

How to Use Soundex: http://obituarieshelp.org/blog/?p=505

Nevada Genealogical Organizations and Archives

Genealogical resources include not only records, but the organizations that house them, or can direct you to them. These institutions include: *Archives, Libraries, Genealogical Societies, Family History Centers, Universities, Churches, and Museums.*

Following are links to their websites, their physical addresses, and a summary of the records you can find there.

Archives and Libraries

Nevada State Library and Archives – marriage and divorce records, Native American Census Rolls, Civil War Muster Rolls, historical newspaper index, probate records, estate records, military service cards for WWI, WWII, Vietnam and Korean wars

Division of Archives and Records
100 North Steward Street
Carson City, NV 89701-4285
Tel: 800-922-2880 (in-state)
State Archives Research Room: 775.684.3310
Fax: 775-684-3311

Nevada State Library and Archives : http://nsla.nevadaculture.org/

National Archives-Pacific Sierra Region – census records, Native American records, Naturalization records, military records, passenger lists

1000 Commodore Dr.
San Bruno, CA 94066-2350
650/238-3501
sanbruno.archives@nara.gov

National Archives-Pacific Sierra Region:
http://www.archives.gov/san-francisco/genealogy.html

University of Nevada, Reno – wealth of historical and genealogical resources including historical newspapers, maps, photographs, women's histories and resources, bibliographies, African American resources, Civil War documentation, and much more

Special Collections
Mail Stop 322
1664 N. Virginia Street
Reno, NV 89557-0044
Telephone: 775-784-4636

University of Nevada, Reno:
http://knowledgecenter.unr.edu/materials/articles/databases.aspx

University of Nevada, Las Vegas - books, pamphlets, posters, serials and periodicals, scrapbooks, archives and manuscripts, maps, oral histories, photographs, video and audio tapes.

Special Collections
4505 Maryland Parkway
Box 457001
Las Vegas, NV 89154-7001
Telephone: (702) 895-2286

University of Nevada, Las Vegas:
http://www.library.unlv.edu/speccol/

Nevada Genealogical and Historical Societies

Genealogical and historical societies have access to extensive catalogues of genealogical data. They are also able to offer expert guidance for genealogical researchers. Many members are professional genealogists who are most willing to share their expertise in finding ancestors.

Nevada Historical Society – variety of historical resources including historical photograph and manuscript colledtions

1650 North Virginia Street
Reno, NV 89503
Telephone: 775-688-1190
Fax: 775-688-2917

Nevada Historical Society: http://museums.nevadaculture.org/

Nevada State Genealogical Society – research support and other genealogical resources for Nevada

Mailing Address:
P.O. Box 20666
Reno, NV 89515-0666

Nevada State Genealogical Society:
http://www.rootsweb.com/~nvsgs/

Nevada Mailing Lists

Mailing lists are internet based facilities that use email to distribute a single message to all who subscribe to it. When information on a particular surname, new records, or any other important genealogy information related to the mailing list topic becomes available, the subscribers are alerted to it. Joining a mailing list is an excellent way to stay up to date on Nevada genealogy research topics. Rootsweb have an extensive listing of **Nevada Mailing Lists** on a variety of topics.

Nevada Mailing Lists:
http://lists.rootsweb.ancestry.com/index/usa/NV/misc.html

Nevada Message Boards

A message board is another internet based facility where people can post questions about a specific genealogy topic and have it answered by other genealogists. If you have questions about a surname, record type, or research topic, you can post your question and other researchers and genealogists will help you with the answer. Be sure to check back regularly, as the answers are not emailed to you. The Nevada message boards at **Rootsweb** are completely free to use.

Rootsweb:
http://boards.rootsweb.com/localities.northam.usa.states/mb.ashx

Nevada Newspapers and Periodicals

Many genealogy periodicals and historical newspapers contain reprinted copies of family genealogies, transcripts of family Bible records, information about local records and archives, census indexes, church records, queries, land records, obituaries, court records, cemetery records, and wills. The following sites have historical Nevada newspapers and periodicals that you can search online or on-site.

Nevada State Library and Archives – Historical newspaper index 1865-1866, 1879-1881, 1885-86

Division of Archives and Records
100 North Steward Street
Carson City, NV 89701-4285
Tel: 800-922-2880 (in-state)
State Archives Research Room: 775.684.3310
Fax: 775-684-3311

Nevada State Library and Archives:
http://nsla.nevadaculture.org/dmdocuments/appeal_index.pdf

University of Nevada, Reno - over 2,200 historic Nevada newspapers from 1759- present

Special Collections
Mail Stop 322
1664 N. Virginia Street
Reno, NV 89557-0044
Telephone: 775-784-4636

University of Nevada, Reno:
http://knowledgecenter.unr.edu/materials/articles/databases.aspx

GenealogyBank.com – free searchable database of Nevada newspaper archives, 1864–1922

GenealogyBank.com: http://www.genealogybank.com/gbnk/newspapers/explore/USA/Nevada/

Library of Congress Digital Newspaper Directory – free searchable database of historical U.S. newspapers dating from 1690-present

Library of Congress Digital Newspaper Directory: http://chroniclingamerica.loc.gov/search/titles/

The Online Books Page – links to historical Nevada books and periodicals available for viewing online, dating from mid-16th century

The Online Books Page: http://onlinebooks.library.upenn.edu

NewspaperArchive.com – largest online database of historical newspapers in the world.

NewspaperArchive.com: http://newspaperarchive.com/

Nevada Maps and Gazetteers

Maps are an integral part of genealogical research. They help us to locate landmarks, towns, cities, parishes, states, provinces, waterways and roads and streets. They also help us to determine when and where boundary changes might have taken place, and give us a visualization of the area we're researching in.

For locating place names, a gazetteer is the best possible resource for any genealogist. Gazetteers are also sometimes called "place name dictionaries", and can help you to locate the area in which you need to conduct research. Below are links to the maps and gazetteers for research in Nevada.

Peabody GNIS Service – Nevada:
http://peabody.research.yale.edu/cgi-bin/Query.GNIS?ST=Nevada&SU=1

Color Landform Atlas – Nevada:
http://fermi.jhuapl.edu/states/nv_0.html

1985 U.S. Atlas: http://www.livgenmi.com/1895/NV/

Nevada Hometown Locator: http://nevada.hometownlocator.com

Nevada City Directories

.

City directories are similar to telephone directories in that they list the residents of a particular area. The difference though is what is important to genealogists, and that is they pre-date telephone directories. You can find an ancestor's information such as their street address, place of employment, occupation, or the name of their spouse. A one-stop-shop for finding city directories in Nevada is the **Nevada Online Historical Directories** which contains a listing of every available online historical directory related to Nevada.

Nevada Online Historical Directories:
https://sites.google.com/site/onlinedirectorysite/Home/usa/nv

Nevada State Library and Archives – wide variety of city directories and histories from around the state

Division of Archives and Records
100 North Steward Street
Carson City, NV 89701-4285
Tel: 800-922-2880 (in-state)
State Archives Research Room: 775.684.3310
Fax: 775-684-3311

Nevada State Library and Archives: http://nsla.nevadaculture.org/

Nevada Genealogical Records

<u>Birth, Death, Marriage and Divorce Records</u> – Also known as vital records, birth, death, and marriage certificates are the most basic, yet most important records attached to your ancestor. The reason for their importance is that they not only place your ancestor in a specific place at a definite time, but potentially connect the individual to other relatives. Below is a list of repositories and websites where you can find Nevada vital records.

Birth and death records were not kept in Nevada until 1887. Birth and death records from 1887 to the present are recorded in each county, either in the office of the **County Recorder or County Health Officer**.

County Recorder or County Health Officer:
http://nsla.nevadaculture.org/index.php?option=com_content&task=view&id=1217&Itemid=486

Nevada State Office of Vital Statistics - birth and death records from 1911 to the present for all counties, marriage and divorce records from 1968 to the present

Office of Vital Records
4150 Technology Way, Suite 104
Carson City, Nevada 89706
Telephone: 775-684-4242
Fax: 775-684-4156

Nevada State Office of Vital Statistics: http://health.nv.gov/vs.htm

Nevada State Library and Archives - marriages and divorces for Carson County, Utah and Nevada territories, 1856-1862, marriage records for Douglas, Lyon, Ormsby, Storey and Washoe Counties for 1862-1900

Division of Archives and Records
100 North Steward Street
Carson City, NV 89701-4285
Tel: 800-922-2880 (in-state)
State Archives Research Room: 775.684.3310
Fax: 775-684-3311

Nevada State Library and Archives:
http://nsla.nevadaculture.org/index.php?option=com_content&view=article&id=587&Itemid=513

Family Search has the following indexes which can be searched online for free:

Nevada, County Birth and Death Records, 1871-1992:
https://familysearch.org/search/collection/2053817

Nevada, County Marriages, 1862-1993:
https://familysearch.org/search/collection/1943751

Nevada, Marriage Index, 1956-2005:
https://familysearch.org/search/collection/1949338

Census Reports

Census records are among the most important genealogical documents for placing your ancestor in a particular place at a specific time. Like BDM records, they can also lead you to other ancestors, particularly those who were living under the authority of the head of household.

Federal census records for Nevada exist from 1870–1940 and can be found at:

National Archives-Pacific Sierra Region – Federal population censuses for all States, 1790-1930, Indexes for the 1880, 1900, 1910, and 1920 censuses, Censuses listing residents of American Samoa and Native Americans in California and Nevada

1000 Commodore Dr.
San Bruno, CA 94066-2350
650/238-3501
sanbruno.archives@nara.gov

National Archives-Pacific Sierra Region:
http://www.archives.gov/san-francisco/genealogy.html

National Archives – Federal census Schedules for all states, 1790-1940

8601 Adelphi Road
College Park, MD 20740-6001
Tel: 1-866-272-6272

National Archives: http://www.archives.gov/research/census/

The **Free Census Project** has transcribed many Nevada indexes and new material is added daily

Free Census Project: http://usgwcensus.org/cenfiles/nv.htm

Access Genealogy – Nevada county census records from 1870-1930

Access Genealogy:
http://www.accessgenealogy.com/census/nevada-census-records.htm

African American Census Schedules Online – slave schedules, mortality schedules, slave-owners census

African American Census Schedules Online:
http://www.afrigeneas.com/aacensus/

Native Americans in Census Records (US National Archives):
http://www.archives.gov/research/census/native-americans/

Nevada Church Records

Church and synagogue records are a valuable resource, especially for baptisms, marriages, and burials that took place before 1900. You will need to at least have an idea of your ancestor's religious denomination, and in most cases you will have to visit a brick and mortar establishment to view them.

Most church records are kept by the individual church, although in some denominations, records are placed in a regional archive or maintained at the diocesan level. Local Historical Societies are sometimes the repository for the state's older church records. Below are links archives that maintain church records, as well as a few databases that can be viewed online.

The **Family History Library** contains many church records from a variety of denominations on microfilm.

Family History Library:
http://familysearch.org/learn/wiki/en/Family_History_Library

Central Repositories for Denominational Records

Church of Jesus Christ of Latter-day Saints (Mormons)

Early Mormon Church records for Nevada can be found on film located at the LDS Family History Library in Salt Lake City and can be searched via the **Family History Library Catalog**

Family History Library Catalog:
https://familysearch.org/eng/Library/FHLC/frameset_fhlc.asp

Methodist

United Methodist Archives Center

Drew University Library
PO Box 127
Madison, NJ 07940-0127
Phone: (973) 408-3189
Fax: (973) 408-3909
E-mail: gcah@gcah.org

United Methodist Archives Center:
http://www.gcah.org/site/pp.aspx?c=ghKJI0PHIoE&b=3590193

Protestant Episcopal - records for the Nevada Diocese from 1862 to
1969

The Nevada Historical Society
1650 N. Virginia Street
Reno, NV 89503-1799
Phone: (775) 688-1190
Fax: (775) 688-2917

The Nevada Historical Society: http://museums.nevadaculture.org/

Roman Catholic

Diocese of Las Vegas
Chancery Office
336 Cathedral Way
Las Vegas, NV 89109
Phone: (702) 735-3500
Fax: (702) 735-8941

Mailing Address:
P.O. Box 18316
Reno, NV 89114-8316

Diocese of Las Vegas: http://www.lasvegas-
diocese.org/Home.shtml

Diocese of Reno
290 S. Arlington
Reno, NV 89501-1713
Archives Phone: (775) 326-9440
Fax (775) 348-8619

Diocese of Reno: http://www.renodiocese.org/

Nevada Military Records

More than 40 million Americans have participated in some time of war service since America was colonized. The chance of finding your ancestor amongst those records is exceptionally high. Military records can even reveal individuals who never actually served, such as those who registered for the two World Wars but were never called to duty.

Below are a number of links to websites and archives that contain Nevada military records.

Nevada State Library and Archives – Civil War Muster Rolls Index, WWI, WWII, Vietnam, and Korean War service cards

Division of Archives and Records
100 North Steward Street
Carson City, NV 89701-4285
Tel: 800-922-2880 (in-state)
State Archives Research Room: 775.684.3310
Fax: 775-684-3311

Nevada State Library and Archives:
http://nsla.nevadaculture.org/index.php?option=com_content&task=view&id=1478&Itemid=418

National Archives-Pacific Sierra Region – Revolutionary war military service records

1000 Commodore Dr.
San Bruno, CA 94066-2350
650/238-3501
sanbruno.archives@nara.gov

National Archives-Pacific Sierra Region:
http://www.archives.gov/san-francisco/genealogy.html

US Department of Veterans Affairs Nationwide Gravesite Locator – includes information on veterans and their family members buried in veterans and military cemeteries having a government grave marker.

US Department of Veterans Affairs Nationwide Gravesite Locator: http://gravelocator.cem.va.gov/

You may also find your ancestor's military records in the following databases:

United States General Index to Pension Files, 1861-1934: https://familysearch.org/search/collection/1919699

United States Index to Service Records, War with Spain, 1898: https://familysearch.org/search/collection/1919583

United States Index to Indian Wars Pension Files, 1892-1926 – military pension records of soldiers who fought in the Indian Wars between 1817 and 1898

United States Index to Indian Wars Pension Files, 1892-1926: https://familysearch.org/search/collection/1979427

United States Registers of Enlistments in the U.S. Army, 1798-1914 - index of men who enlisted in the United States Army, 1798-1914.

United States Registers of Enlistments in the U.S. Army, 1798-1914: https://familysearch.org/search/collection/1880762

United States Mexican War Pension Index, 1887-1926 link to: https://familysearch.org/search/collection/1979390

Civil War Soldiers Service Records - Service records for both Union and Confederate soldiers indexed by soldier's name, rank, and unit.

Civil War Soldier Service Records: http://go.fold3.com/civilwar_records/

Nevada Cemetery Records

As convenient as it is to search cemetery records online, keep in mind that there are a few disadvantages over visiting a cemetery in person. They are:

- Tombstone information is not always accurately transcribed
- The arrangement of the graves in a cemetery can be crucial as family members are often buried next to each other or in the same grave. This arrangement is not always preserved in the alphabetical indexes that are found online.

With that information in mind, the following websites have databases that can be searched online for Nevada Cemetery records.

Nevada Tombstone Transcription Project - death and burial records

Nevada Tombstone Transcription Project:
http://www.usgwtombstones.org/nevada/nevada.html

African American Cemeteries Online – African American, slave, and Native American cemetery records

African American Cemeteries Online:
http://africanamericancemeteries.com/

Access Genealogy – Nevada cemetery record transcriptions

Access Genealogy :
http://www.accessgenealogy.com/cemetery/nevada-cemetery-records.htm

Find a Grave – over 100 million grave records can be searched on this site. Search can be conducted by name, location, or cemetery name.

Find a Grave: http://www.findagrave.com/

Interment.net - A free online database containing approximately 4 million cemetery records from around the world.

Interment.net: http://www.interment.net/

Billion Graves – as the name implies, you can search a billion records including headstone photos, transcriptions, cemetery records, and grave locations.

Billion Graves:
http://billiongraves.com/pages/search/index.php#cemetery

Nevada Obituaries

Obituaries can reveal a wealth about our ancestor and other relatives. You can search our **Nevada Newspaper Obituaries Listings** from hundreds of Nevada newspapers online for free.

Nevada Newspaper Obituaries Listings:
http://obituarieshelp.org/nevada_newspaper_obituaries.html

Nevada Wills and Probate Records

The documents found in a probate packet may include a complete inventory of a person's estate, newspaper entries, witness testimony, a copy of a will, list of debtors and creditors, names of executors or trustees, names of heirs. They can not only tell you about the ancestor you're currently researching, but lead to other ancestors.

Jurisdiction of probates in Nevada is held by the **Clerk of the District Court** in each county.

Clerk of the District Court:
http://supreme.nvcourts.gov/Find_a_Court/District_Courts/

Nevada Probate Court actions before 1861 were recorded in Utah Territory courts. The majority, if not all, of the records from this period are now at the:

Nevada State Library and Archives

Division of Archives and Records
100 North Steward Street
Carson City, NV 89701-4285
Tel: 800-922-2880 (in-state)
State Archives Research Room: 775.684.3310
Fax: 775-684-3311

Nevada State Library and Archives:
http://nsla.nevadaculture.org/index.php?option=com_content&view=article&id=587&Itemid=513#public

Nevada Immigration and Naturalization Records

The naturalization process generated many types of records, including petitions, declarations of intention, and oaths of allegiance. These records can provide family historians with information such as a person's birth date and place of birth, immigration year, marital status, spouse information, occupation, witnesses' names and addresses, and more.

National Archives-Pacific Sierra Region – passenger arrivals for San Francisco, Indexes to naturalization records from Federal courts in Reno

1000 Commodore Dr.
San Bruno, CA 94066-2350
650/238-3501
sanbruno.archives@nara.gov

National Archives-Pacific Sierra Region:
http://www.archives.gov/san-francisco/genealogy.html

U.S. National Archives – Immigration and Naturalization records, 1787-1993

U.S. National Archives: http://www.archives.gov/research/guide-fed-records/groups/085.html

Nevada Native American Records

Nevada State Library and Archives –Native American Census Rolls

Division of Archives and Records
100 North Steward Street
Carson City, NV 89701-4285
Tel: 800-922-2880 (in-state)
State Archives Research Room: 775.684.3310
Fax: 775-684-3311

Nevada State Library and Archives:
http://nsla.nevadaculture.org/index.php?option=com_content&task=view&id=1125&Itemid=418

National Archives-Pacific Sierra Region – Censuses listing Native Americans in California and Nevada, records documenting the removal of Cherokees and other tribes included in Oklahoma Removal, ca. 1900

1000 Commodore Dr.
San Bruno, CA 94066-2350
650/238-3501
sanbruno.archives@nara.gov

National Archives-Pacific Sierra Region:
http://www.archives.gov/san-francisco/genealogy.html

Access Genealogy – Nevada Native American census records, tribal histories, and much more

Access Genealogy: http://www.accessgenealogy.com/native/nevada-indian-tribes.htm

U.S. National Archives - information on American Indians who maintained their ties to Federally-recognized Tribes (1830-1970).

U.S. National Archives: http://www.archives.gov/research/native-americans/

Records of the Bureau of Indian Affairs (BIA):
http://www.archives.gov/research/guide-fed-
records/groups/075.html

American Indians Records Repository - records dating from the
1700s including trust, education and other historic Indian Affairs
records

American Indian Records Repository
Meritex Enterprises
17501 West 98th Street
Lenexa, KS 66219
Phone: 913-888-0601

American Indians Records Repository:
http://www.doi.gov/ost/records_mgmt/american-indian-records-
repository.cfm

Missing Matriarchs – Resources for Researching Female Nevada Ancestors

Looking for female ancestors requires an adjustment of how we view traditional records sources. A woman's identity was often under that of her husband, and often individual records for them can be difficult to locate. The following resources are effective in locating female ancestors in Nevada where traditional records may not reveal them.

Bibliographies

- *A Lady in Boomtown: Miners and Manners on the Nevada Frontier,* Marjorie and Hugh Brown (University of Nevada Press, 1991)
- *To Clothe Nevada Women, 1860-1920,* Janet I. Loverin (Nevada State Museum, 1990)
- *Quilts in Nevada,* Nevada Historical Society (The Society, 1994)
- *Women of the Sierra,* Anne Seagraves (Wesanne Publications, 1990)

Selected Resources for Nevada Women's History

Nevada Women's Archives
James R. Dickinson Library
University of Nevada – Las Vegas
4504 Maryland Parkway
Box 457010
Las Vegas, NV 89154-7010

Nevada Women's Archives
University Library
University of Nevada – Reno
Reno, NV 89557-0044

Nevada Women's History Project
1048 N. Sierra, #A
Reno, NV 89503

Common Nevada Surnames

The following surnames are among the most common in Nevada and are also being currently researched by other genealogists. If you find your surname here, there is a chance that some research has already been performed on your ancestor.

Agee, Agmata, Allen, Allen, Austin, Baker, Barries, Batiste, Bell, Bennett, Blake, Bradley, Broadnax, Brock, Brown, Burke, Butler, Campbell, Campbell, Carr, Carroll, Carter, Chata, Christian, Clark, Clayton, Cole, Coleman, Cooper, Crutchfield, Daugherty, Davis, Dennis, Dieudenne, Diggs, Downer, Dozier, Dumas, Enette, Ennis, Fallon, Ficklin, Furnace, Gaston, Gibson, Glass, Golden, Grant, Gray, Green, Greene, Grigsby, Hall, Hamilton, Harper, Harris, Hartwell, Hawkins, Hayes, Heck, Hicks, Hirsch, Hobbs, Hodges, Howard, Ishmael, Jack, Jacks, Jackson, Jacobs, Johanson, Johnson, Jones, Knutson, Lafayette, LaGarde, Thompson, Lamb, Latham, Lea, Lee, Lynch, Mack, Madden, Maddox, Magee, Maranville, Marks, Marshall, Maxwell, McClain, McCord, McGee, McIntyre, Melendez, Meza, Mitchell, Moore, Murray, Owens, Page, Pantin, Parker, Pitts, Presiado, Prichard, Pugh, Ramos, Ree, Reed, Reese, Richardson, Richey, Ritz, Ritz, Robinson, Rosenberg, Sayles, Shepard, Simon, Slack, Sledge, Smart, Smith, Snowden, Sowels, Stevens, Sweat, Taylor, Thierry, Thomas, Thompson, Thrower, Tootle, Tulluo, Turner, Vargas, Virgil, Walker, Wallace, Ware, Washington, Watkins, Watts, Wayerski, Wayne, White, Wier, Wiley, Wilkins, Wilks, Williams, Williford, Willis, Wilson, Wright, Yancy, Young

About the Author

Gary L. Morris worked from 2009 to 2014 as a professional researcher for a major player in the genealogy field. After tracing his family lineage back to 1683, he found that genealogy could be an expensive undertaking. As such, has decided to publish these helpful guides to share the valuable free information he has discovered during his career to help others trace their family lineages as inexpensively as possible. An avid genealogist himself, he hopes you will find this guide factual, thorough, helpful, and most of all, effective in helping you to find your family members.

Notes

Notes

www.ingramcontent.com/pod-product-compliance
Lightning Source LLC
Chambersburg PA
CBHW072021290526
45787CB00013B/1606